WORD FROM THE EDITOR

A new year approaches, bringing a new decade along with it. Resolutions and promises aside, something new is almost here. We can choose to keep our course and change nothing, or we can completely turn our lives in a new direction. Either way, one foot has to step in front of the other. But a date on a calendar doesn't have to dictate change, it can only make for a cleaner break. In these pages you'll find the words of those dealing with newness and what it all means, but the question that will remain at the end of these pages is this: Where are you headed?

5	SOMETHING NEW
10	IN THE MIRROR
12	CARNAL LUST
14	THE VICE COLUMN: A LIST OF NEW VICES TO TRY
17	NEW TO YOU
18	THERAPIST HUNTING
20	I'VE DECIDED TO BE BEAUTIFUL
21	ABSOLUTE MAGNITUDE
22	YELLOW DIAMONDS

SOMETHING NEW
JOSEPHINE JAEL JIMENEZ

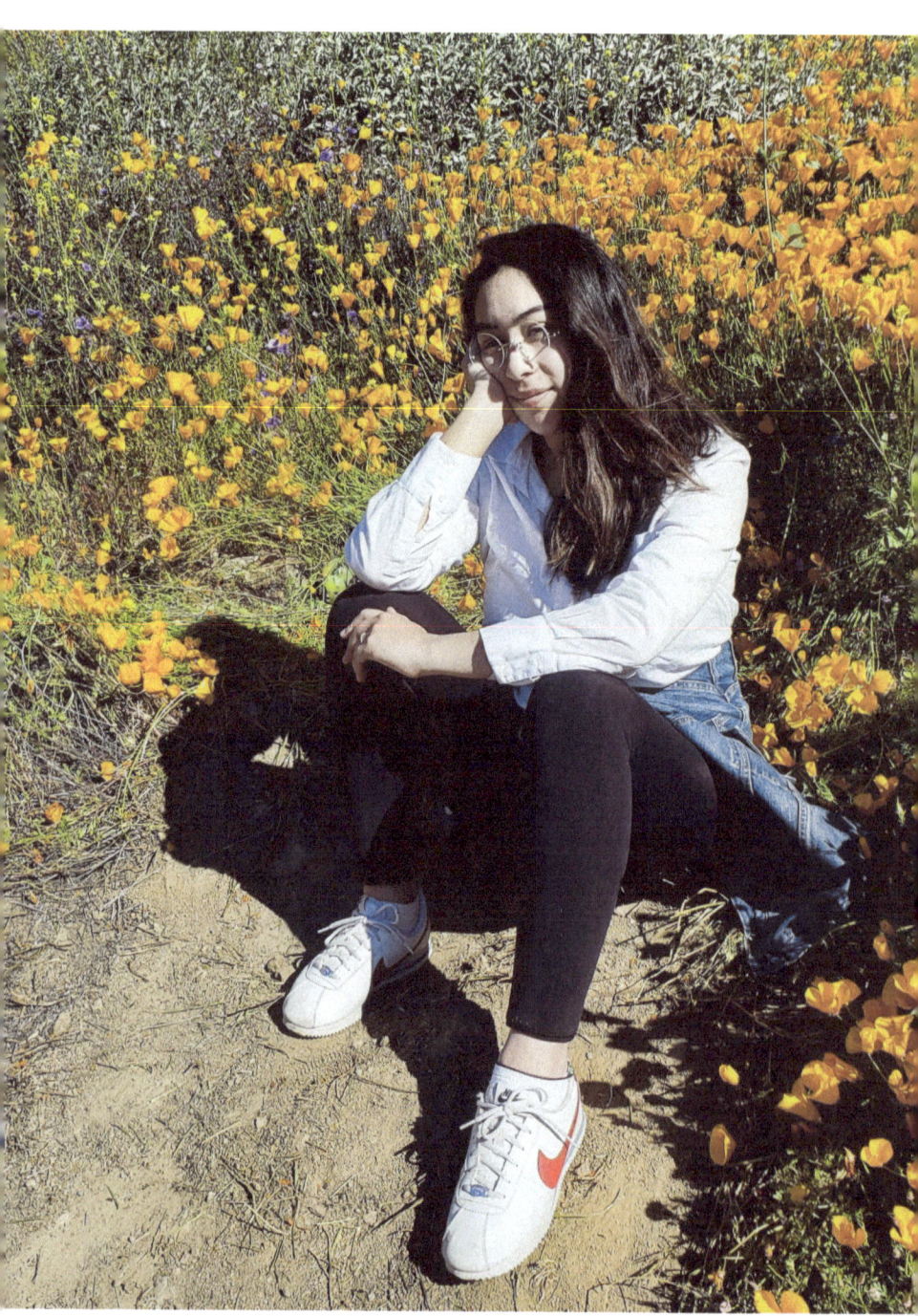

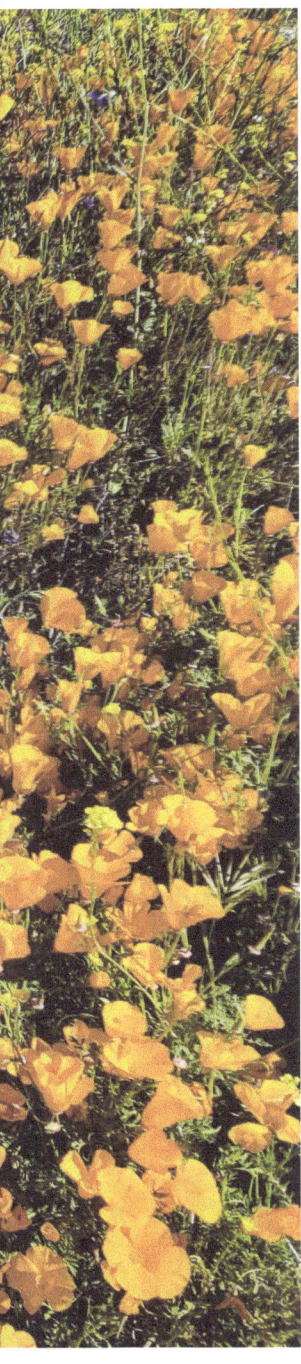

I'm not a different person when the clock strikes midnight at the end of another year, not even at the end of another decade. Nothing about me feels different. Nothing about the world feels brighter or newer or more hopeful than the last day of the last year. It all feels the same, only now I have to practice writing the date because that really is different.

People and places don't really change. They don't make a complete 180. The past is still always there to haunt the people and places that try to be someone or something that they're not. Change is generally inevitable, but it's not fate or written in the stars somewhere in the universe. Change is molded and forced, but it never gets rid of the underlying soul of someone or something. That stays the same.

We're born innocent with a breath and a cry into a world that can't wait to change us. Our parents want to mold us into the person they could never be and each side of every coin wants us to join their team and uphold their ideals. From day one we're bombarded with people and institutions that crave our acceptance and our loyalty and we give in to some because we can't feed or care for ourselves. We have to pledge ourselves to someone or something to survive.

Most of our parents mean well, but then again some don't. They all make us grow up, whether slowly or way too fast, and they all exist somewhere, whether we know them or not. Two people had to splice their DNA to create us. We were born from two halves to create a whole new person and sometimes we don't get the desired parts of selves our guardians wanted us to

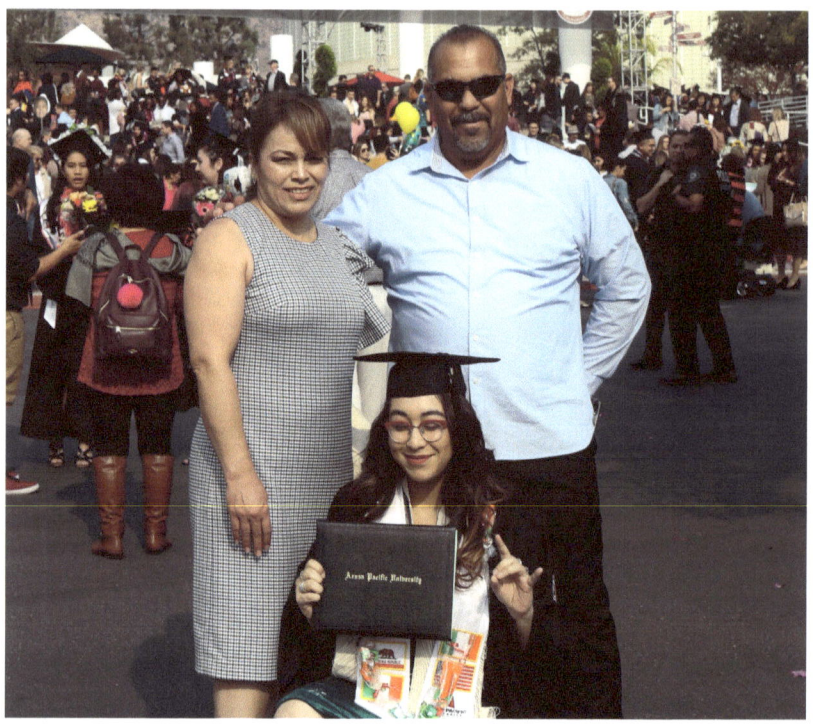

have. Some of us are exactly like our biological parents and they end up not liking that so much either.

My soul is the same, but my mother changed me slowly slowly slowly and made me grow up way too fast because I was born with her stubbornness. The more I age and the more I interact with my mother, the more it becomes apparent that she has resented me for so long because I am the better version of her in almost every way. I'm the person she wanted to be, but couldn't be. So she hit me.

It's a weird relationship I have with my mother, the one who would hit me out of anger and who would say terrible things to me when I was misbehaving or existing in a way that was opposed to her will. I have to forgive her everyday and I have to be patient with the fact that she hasn't changed all that much since I left her house, but mostly I'm grateful for who she was to me in the most abstract sense.

My mother shouldn't have hit me the way she did and she shouldn't have said the things she said. She shouldn't have kept food from me when she was angry. But all those things made me more independent, more appreciative of the things that I have, and much more willing to share what I can as much as I can. Over the years of abuse, what my mother wanted was to break a glazed jar so she could put back the pieces in the pattern that she had originally set out to create, but instead my soul held true to who I was born to be: myself. I never became the person she wanted me to be and most of

> "...I became a person I can be proud of and any other life wouldn't have molded me into who I am now and I love who I am now."

the time she doesn't try, but even when she does, the pieces that fell off over the years of her breaking me down have laid out a clear, sharp boundary she cannot cross. Maybe that's sad, the fact that my mother can't come close to the soul I was born with, but it's peaceful. My soul finally rests, unchanged. The parts my mother gave to me changed to protect that rest.

Sometimes I'm asked if I would change the life I had if I could and most of the time people are surprised when I say that I wouldn't touch it. It's perfect the way it is because even after the abuse, I became a person I can be proud of and any other life wouldn't have molded me into who I am now and I love who I am now.

But other people change you and try to break you, too. Friendships come and go, some with the wind and some with a bang. Each one lays a finger on your soul and decides whether it likes what's there or not. And every time a friend leaves, there's an ache for what once was, for the touch that was meant to decide whether to stay or go.

Some people stick around to find out what makes up who you are. They try to understand your bad parts as much as your good parts and they put enough effort and care into you to stick around for a long time. Some friendships are passionate and burn out at the first sight of trouble, a love that was never meant to be. Every heartbreak changes you because something was taken from you and you'll always remember when and why they decided to walk away.

Of all the things that can change you, there is none more concrete than an education. Whether in a building or in a book or in a far off place or in the walls of your home. The presence of knowledge will either make you evolve or it will solidify who you thought you were. Both changes that are noble and true. For me it was college.

I found new ways to express myself and I found people who made me fall in love and who taught me how to love. In four years, I've never changed more and became more of who I was. I've never fought harder for myself and others and that was an education in and of itself. It was a measurable amount of time and it was a formative amount of time because I was forced to come to terms with the fact that the people who grew up differently than me weren't an abstract idea I could ignore, they were real flesh and bones and they walked and talked whether I wanted them to or not. They taught me whether I wanted them to or not, in the lecture hall and in the dorm hall. College is where you learn to be tolerant or intolerant and I'd like to think I learned the former much better than the latter. Everyday was something new during those four years.

During that time was also when I learned how fervently I loved being alone. My mind was great company and my thoughts were great guests.

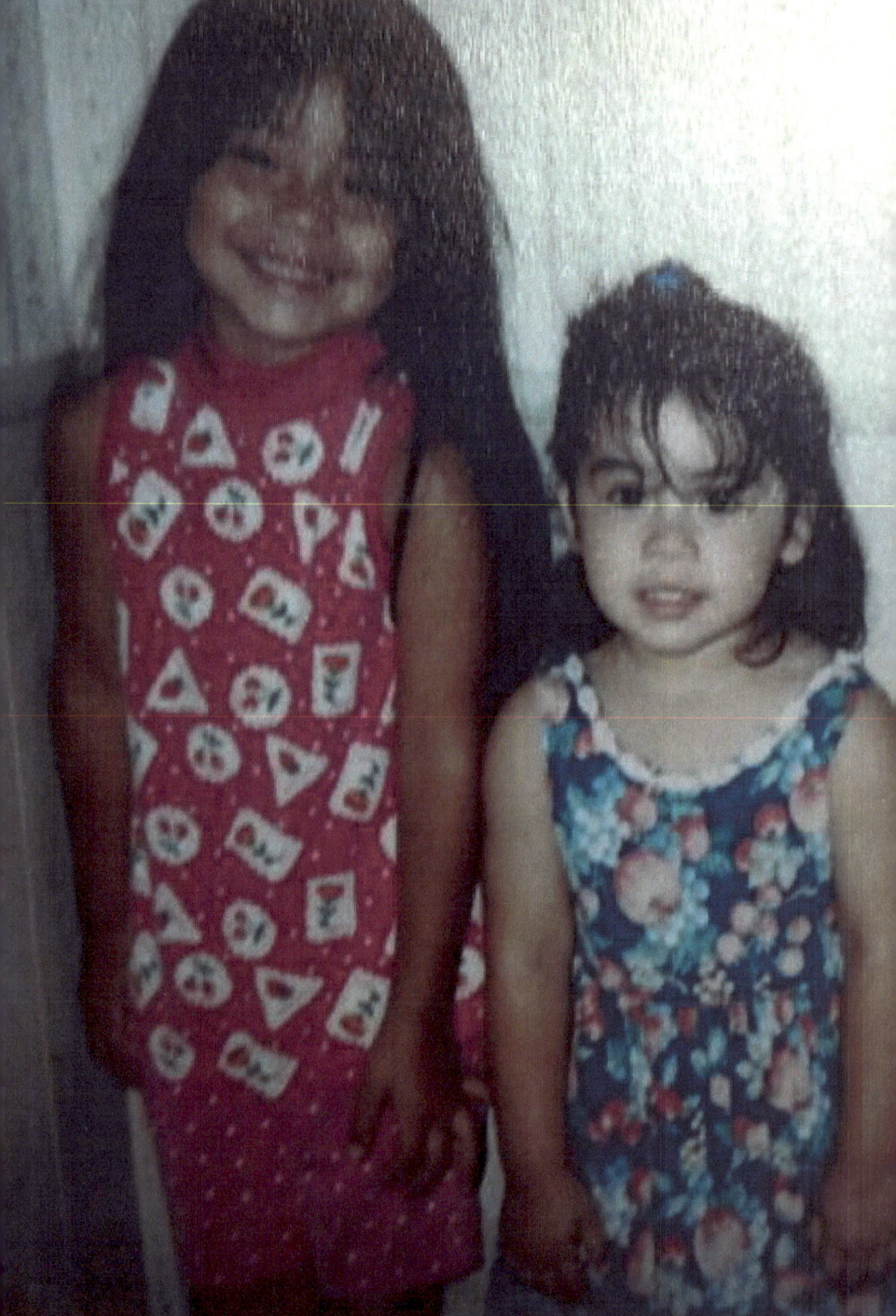

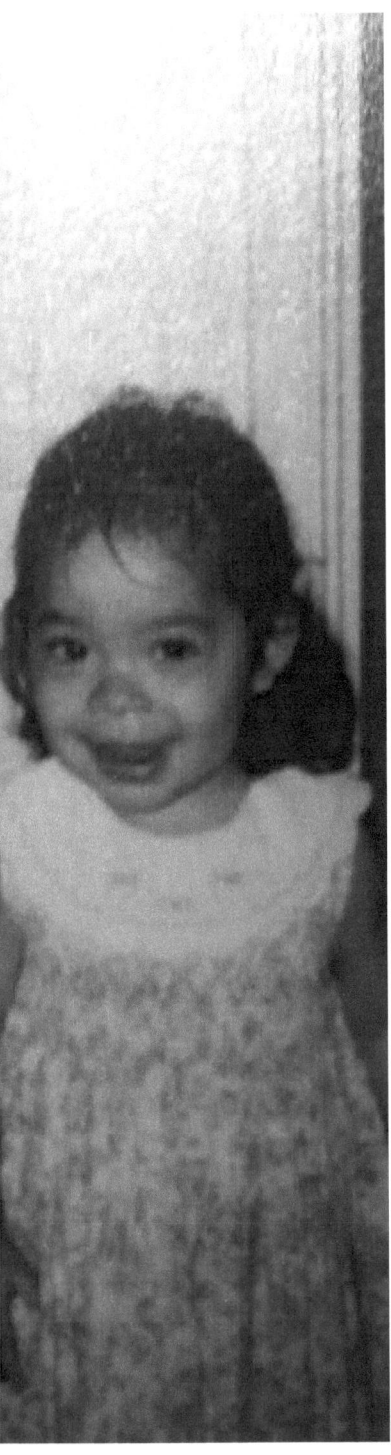

They came and went and came when they were called. In my head is where I evolve the most, where we all do I suppose. It's where change becomes permanent or where the permanent changes we've made are questioned. In my solitude, I find change can hold and be warmed by.

But sometimes those thoughts lead to changes I never knew would come. It was in my head that I lost my God for a brief period of time. In my head I think of death as blackness, as nothing and my heart races and my breath quickens and I stop being able to feel God until suddenly I do again. After a while of those short episodes, God felt distant because the people that said they loved him didn't love me for one reason or another and they didn't love the people Jesus said they were supposed to love and it all became so confusing until it was just so easy to walk away. Losing God changes people more than they care to say, but I think I've found him again. Even still, it's not the same. It's a new relationship I haven't figured out yet. It's not innocent like it used to be and I'm not quite sure what that means at the moment. It's all new.

All these changes and the ones to come have nothing to do with turning a calendar page and only a few of them are distinctly time based at all. They're all a blur, only evidenced by the concreteness of who I am now. But even this version of me, that exists right this second could be gone the next or the next or tomorrow. Something new will always come to lead me to the next version of who I will be until someday, it won't. Until then, all this change feels good.

IN THE MIRROR
ASHLEE POLAREK

She pulled a cozy sweater over a tiny tank top completing her look, "Sexy Fall" is what she called it. She wore a leather skirt, impractical for the weather outside but alluring. With her heels on she looked like a librarian that every man fantasized about fucking.

"It's Friday night. Why aren't you going out?"

"You know it's not my thing."

A chuckle fell from her lips as she fluffed her hair, "None of this shit is your thing."

"Whatever." I rolled over and transitioned into downward-dog.

"You're really going to stay home, listen to podcasts and do yoga?"

"Yes. Going out costs money. Plus, I don't have anyone to go out with."

"Yourself? How about that? Meet someone, go on a fucking date."

"I like to be alone."

"Liar." She perfected her lipstick, a pretty berry pink, one I'd be far too afraid to wear.

"Fuck you."

"You're so full of it. You tell everyone you prefer to be alone. It's not true. You crave interaction. love, someone to hold you at night, to pull you into his lap and prove to everyone you're spoken for... that you're his."

I gave up on my yoga, collapsing on the floor and looking at her in the mirror. Angry tears threating my composure.

"You're hot you know. It's not like you're some beast that men don't want. You just don't listen when people tell you that you're pretty."

"I'm safe here."

"Fuck safe. Be free. It's what you want. You're too scared to actually be yourself. To open up to someone, to be vulnerable. To tell the truth about who you are and what you want." Her eyes met mine in the mirror, reflecting confidence in her sure and serious expression. "You're afraid of being trapped but you've trapped yourself in a pretty little cage. The bars are your fears, the lies you've told yourself and the idiotic sentiment that you're not worthy of happiness."

"Shut up," I growled slamming my fist into the mirror, watching as the glass shook her image from the frame and she disappeared like smoke. I was left staring back at myself tears falling down my cheeks. I was alone in the room trapped in a beautiful little cage of my own design and that's when I decided to be beautiful.

CARNAL LUST

i keep one star for every name on my list
like tiny globes on my shoulders

night only feels good when i measure
missives, jagged edges, crashed cosmos

i drowsy dream, on the back patio
palm trees dotting my skin:

i am careless, i just want to be wanted.

- stephanie valente

Let me have this one
for all my effort
the years of yearning
the learning
growing through
I've made room
maybe you can
leave the door
unlocked

- Kate Hilderbrandt

THE VICE COLUMN

A List of New Vices to Try

Josephine Jael Jimenez

Baking

Sweets aren't very good for you, but sharing them with those around you definitely is. You'll learn something new and you'll make your neighbors feel like you give a shit about them while trying to get all the stuff you make from your new hobby out of your house. Win/win.

Showering

Really think about the showers you take. Instead of taking one every day, try every other day. You'll save tons of water and your skin won't be as dry because no one needs to shower every fucking day. For those of you who don't shower regularly, you should start showering. We can smell you.

Drinking

Drink more fucking water. All the water you save from not showering every day should be going down your throat. You'll feel better and you'll look better and you won't die. God, you should have seriously learned this by now.

Reading

Pick up a fucking book for once or reading a newspaper. Novels are fun and non-fiction books are informative. And stop watching racists "news" pundits on YouTube. READ THE NEWS FROM CREDIBLE NEWS SOURCES. Those assholes on YouTube don't know what they're fucking talking about and you'll realize that when you start learning from all the new books you're reading.

Sex

Concensual sex is awesome. So stop making lame excuses and have sex with your committed partner. Not only will it elevate your mood, but it will strengthen your relationship. Maybe they'll even be grateful enough to bake you a cheesecake from their new baking habit. For all you single people, treat yourself sexually however you desire. Except for rape. Your new vice should definitely be to turn yourself in to police if you like raping people.

Gardening

There are plenty of houseplants on the market that require very minimal care, but having a plant in your house is kind of cool and can kind of clean your air. If you have outside space, try growing fruit or vegetables or herbs. Fresh food hits different.

Meditating

Take a second or a million to just chill out and do nothing. Center yourself and give your brain a break from constant stimulation. Thank me later.

Eating

Eat a fucking vegetable for once. Grow one and then eat it. Regularly.

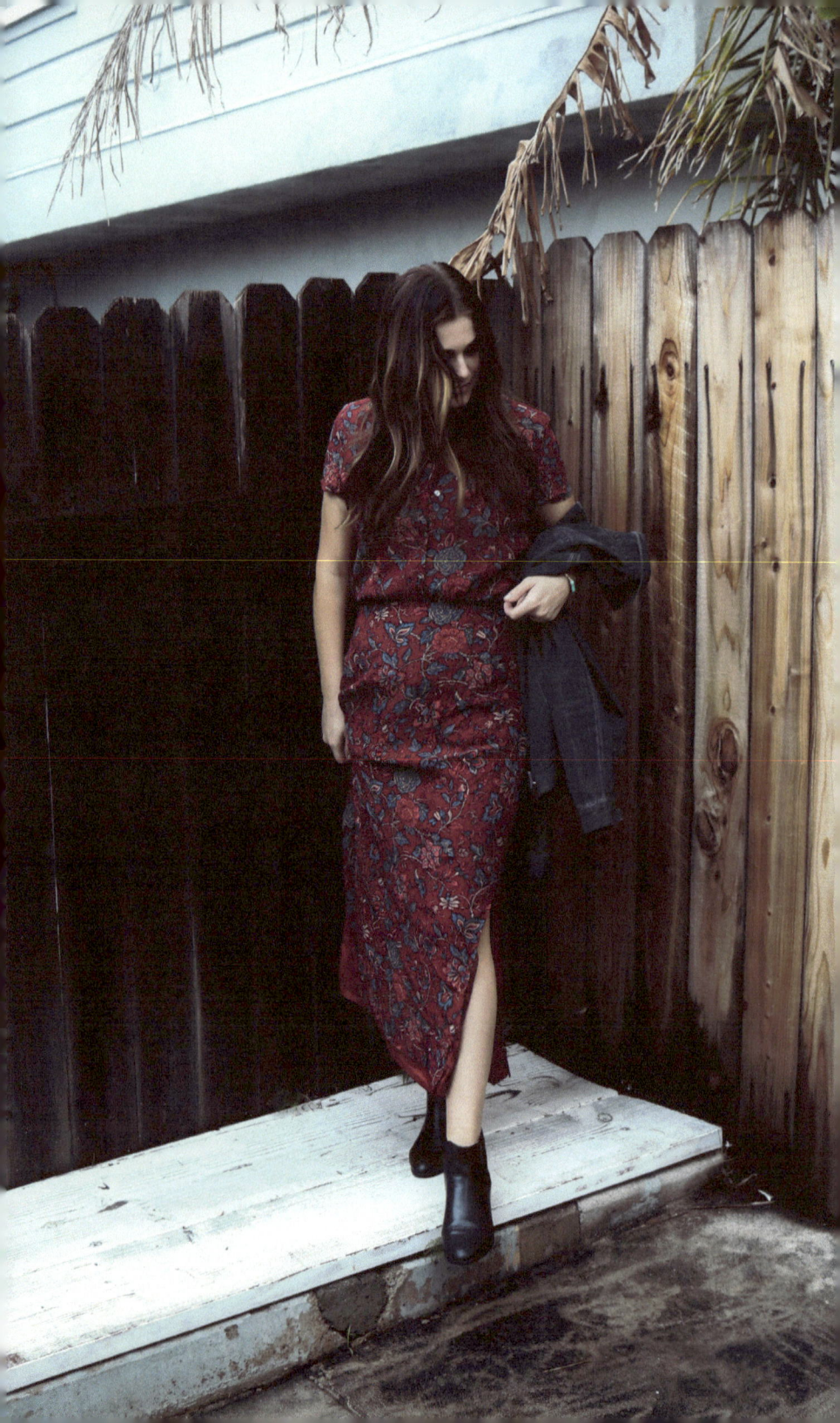

NEW TO YOU
@TRASH.THRIFTED

    Trash Thrifted is a social media based thrift store whose mission is to curate styles for the greater good. Seriously.

    The fashion industry is the 3rd most polluting industry in the world and fast fashion is the reason. We have gotten used to thinking of clothing as temporary, not just in the way we make it, but in the way we wear it. Our closets are full to the brim with clothing we only wear a handul of time and then either throw away or donate to oversaturated stores. Trash exists to make treasures out of your clothes.

    If more people bought second hand clothing, the environment would benefit in huge ways. Less water would be allocated to producing clothing and less microplastic waste from clothing fibers would end up polluting our oceans.

    The women behind Trash, Mahala Rain Hughes Pokorny and Josephine Jael Jimenez know how important the cool factor is. Most other online sellers of second hand good rely on flat lays to sell of merchandise. They use real people to model their clothes because real people will buy and wear their clothes. And with real people prices that are affordable and attainable, these ladies hope to create a quality movement that will have a lasting environmental impact.

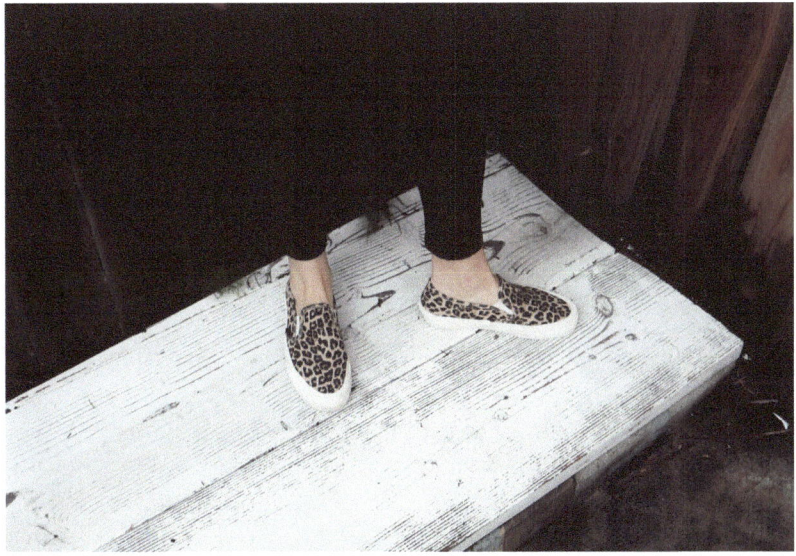

THERAPIST HUNTING

feeling like an anchor
washing over warm water
so long, it stops
feeling like water

that feeling is a mask, comfort
i forget to open the mail, envelopes
slowly curl, unread letters

my anchor dips,
i live by the sea
i am salt, a glass
spirit, full or empty

it's the same, you know

i am blue, teal, & most things
there are glimmers that haven't happened yet

i tell myself: so many e-mails unread
so many strangers to meet
so many stories to turn into crystals
hiding under my bed, inside my teeth

i'll tell them
how you licked the peach juice off my wrists
while i waited for nothing, but
in that sliver of time, it was everything.

- stephanie valente

She will become
softer, melting
into blankets and
burrows for the season
shedding summer skin
in favor of cashmere and
cider, fires to keep her
warm until spring

- Kate Hilderbrandt

I'VE DECIDED TO BE BEAUTIFUL
ASHLEE POLAREK

I've decided to be beautiful.

Like the warrior that guides my soul brave and fierce.

I want the confidence that I put on every morning like a warm coat
To fill my insides. My head. My heart.

I've decided to be beautiful.

Like a blossoming field of flowers relishing in the breeze.

I want the sun that warms my skin to be a radiance felt by others
In my smile or in my embrace.

I've decided to be beautiful.

Like laughter dancing off someone's lips, joy incarnate.

I want my words to be sweet like honey on a spring day
When they pour from my mouth or out on to the page.

I've decided to be beautiful.

Like the Mother Nature powerful and strong.

I want her waves to wash over me,
her waters a guide for the next adventure.

I've decided to be beautiful.

Even if no one else agrees.

Even if everyone agrees.

I've decided to be beautiful.

For me.

ABSOLUTE MAGNITUDE

who wants to be the spirit of the hour?
i only speak with wolves
chant the sky on my arms
i want to pull up the stars
laugh in astrology houses
trying to make peace with foxes
my chipped black nail polish
my boots scraping against the sidewalk
my ribs sighing with ancient history
there are nebulas within me,
stories from the old gods trying to crawl
i'll sing it: if only you'd let me.

- stephanie valente

YELLOW DIAMONDS

imagine a world full of saturday nights
just a neon carnival with no animals,
just people
long nails for daddy, my voice is chiffon
tangible, but at times meaningless
moans
sweaty, embezzlers of affairs
what if the blue-dark stayed forever?
laughing like parlor ghosts in hazelnut
perfume
breasts and hands and waiting

crush the stones, rub the dust all over
my skin.

- stephanie valente

Everything you said to me
I refuse to believe.
In me lived a soul
that some people dream of
and I nourished it
until we became unstoppable,
even when you said
I would amount to nothing
unless I swapped it out
for something new.

- Josephine Jael Jimenez

Ashlee Polarek, @thegreatbigwonder, thegreatbigwonder.com
Kate Hilderbrandt, @seekateinnovate
Stephanie Valente, stephanievalente.com
Trash Thrifted, @trash.thrifted

Josephine Jael Jimenez, Designer & Editor-in-Chief, @josietakestheworld
Young Ignorantes, @youngignorantes, youngignorantes.com

www.ingramcontent.com/pod-product-compliance
Lightning Source LLC
Chambersburg PA
CBHW040350220526
45473CB00009B/2833